Mexican Fiesta!

Publications International, Ltd.

Favorite Brand Name Recipes at www.fbnr.com

Microwave Cooking: Microwave ovens vary in wattage. Use the cooking times as guidelines and check for doneness before adding more time.

Preparation/Cooking Times: Preparation times are based on the approximate amount of time required to assemble the recipe before cooking, baking, chilling or serving. These times include preparation steps such as measuring, chopping and mixing. The fact that some preparations and cooking can be done simultaneously is taken into account. Preparation of optional ingredients and serving suggestions is not included.

table of
contents

ingredients

orn, tomatoes, chili peppers and beans are the foundation ingredients of Mexican food. Besides indigenous ingredients and cooking techniques from the native culture of Mexico, Mexican food was influenced by the arrival of the Spanish to the New World. Mexican food that we enjoy today north of the border has been further modified into spicy-hot Tex-Mex dishes and flavorful Southwestern specialties.

Cooking Mexican food requires very little in the way of specialized equipment, but knowing a few of the foods and food terms can be helpful. Here are some typical ingredients and a few food terms to help you enjoy this colorful and inherently healthful cuisine:

Burrito (burr-EE-toh) A large flour tortilla folded to enclose a variety of fillings such as cooked, shredded meat or chicken, refried beans, shredded cheese, sour cream, lettuce, tomatoes and salsa.

Carnitas (car-NEE-tas) Bits of shredded, cooked pork that are cooked again in pork fat until well browned. Carnitas, or "little meats," is derived from the word *carne*, or "meat." Carnitas are sometimes used to fill burritos.

Chayote (chi-OH-tay) A gourdlike fruit about the size and shape of a pear, but with furrowed, pale green skin. It is served cooked and has a bland flavor, like zucchini.

Chili Pungent pods of the Capsicum family used to flavor foods. There are more than 200 varieties, ranging in heat from mild to blistering. Chili peppers are rich sources of vitamins A and C.

Chorizo (chore-EETZ-zo) A spicy pork sausage used in Mexican and Spanish dishes. Mexican chorizo is made with fresh pork; Spanish chorizo uses smoked pork. To cook Mexican chorizo, removed the casing and crumble it into the pan before frying.

Cilantro

Cilantro (see-LAN-troh) The light green, delicate leaves of the coriander plant, noted for a pungent flavor that some people define as "soapy." It is an acquired taste, not liked by all but loved passionately by some.

Crema (crem-ma) A thick, ripened Mexican cream, similar to American sour cream or French *crème fraîche*.

Empanada (em-pah-NA-duh) Turnovers with either savory or sweet fillings in a pastry crust. An empanada made with a meat and vegetable filling serves as a meal, while smaller turnovers—called *empanaditas*—are usually sweet and served as dessert.

Enchilada (en-chuh-LA-duh) Tortillas rolled around a meat or cheese filling then baked in a casserole.

Flan (FLAHN) A Mexican dessert of custard baked over a layer of caramel.

Spanish Onion

Flauta (FLAU-ta) A corn tortilla tightly rolled around a shredded meat filling, then fried until crisp.

Frijoles (free-HO-lays) The Mexican word for "beans." *Frijoles refritos* are cooked beans that have been mashed with seasonings and fat, then refried.

Avocado

Guacamole (gwah-kah-MOE-lay) Popular dip made with mashed avocados that have been seasoned with lime juice, chili powder, diced tomato, green onion and sometimes cilantro.

Jicama (HICK-uh-muh) A large bulb-shaped vegetable that resembles a potato but has crisp, crunchy white flesh that is eaten raw. For a refreshing treat, dip peeled jicama slices in freshly squeezed lime juice, then sprinkle with chili powder and salt.

Masa (MA-suh) The traditional cornmeal dough used to make tortillas. It is made from dried corn kernels cooked in limewater (water mixed with calcium oxide). The soaked kernels are ground into flour or masa.

Mexican Chocolate A grainy-textured chocolate flavored with almonds, cinnamon and vanilla and sold in round disks. It is used to make hot chocolate and to flavor sauces such as mole.

Mole (MOE-lay) A rich, thick, dark sauce made with onion, garlic, sesame or pumpkin seeds, chilies and chocolate. It is often served over chicken or turkey.

Pico de Gallo (PEE-ko duh-GUY-yo) A salsa or relish made of chopped ingredients such as jicama, oranges, onion, bell peppers, chilies and cucumbers as well as seasonings.

Lime

Piloncillo (pil-on-CEE-yo) Small, hard cones of unrefined sugar, about the color of dark brown sugar and a little stronger in taste. To use, let the cone dissolve in whatever liquid your recipe calls for or grate it into small pieces.

Plantain (PLAN-tihn) A large, firm type of banana used in cooked dishes. Its flavor and texture is close to a potato.

Quesadillas (kay-sa-DEE-yahs) A large flour tortilla spread with savory ingredients such as cheese, cooked beans and salsa, then folded and cooked by broiling or frying.

Queso (KAY-so) The Mexican word for "cheese." *Queso fresco* is a fresh, white cheese similar to farmer cheese. It is also known as *queso blanco* or white cheese.

Tomato

Salsa (SAHL-sah) A fresh or cooked sauce typically made with red tomatoes or green tomatillos seasoned with chilies, onion and cilantro.

Tomatillo (tom-a-TEE-yo) A close relative of the tomato that is green and enclosed in a papery husk. It has a refreshing citrus flavor with hints of apple. It is the basis of *salsa verde* or green sauce.

Tortilla (tor-TEE-ya) An unleavened, round bread that is the staple food of Mexico. They are made from corn or wheat flour and are baked on a griddle. Tortillas are eaten plain or wrapped around fillings.

celebrate
cinco de mayo

FIRE AND ICE

Makes 6 servings

    2 cups vanilla ice milk or low-fat ice cream
    2 teaspoons finely chopped jalapeño pepper*
    1 teaspoon grated lime peel, divided
    1 cup water
    ¼ cup sugar
    1 cup peeled and chopped kiwifruit
    1 tablespoon lime juice
    1 cup fresh raspberries

*Jalapeño peppers can sting and irritate the skin; wear rubber gloves when handling peppers and do not touch eyes. Wash hands after handling.

1. Soften ice milk slightly in small bowl. Stir in jalapeño pepper and ½ teaspoon lime peel. Freeze until firm.

2. Combine water, sugar and remaining ½ teaspoon lime peel in small saucepan; bring to a boil. Boil, uncovered, 5 minutes or until reduced by about one third. Remove from heat and cool to room temperature.

3. Place kiwifruit and lime juice in blender or food processor; process until smooth. Stir in water mixture. Pour through fine strainer to remove kiwifruit seeds and lime peel, pressing liquid through strainer with back of spoon. Refrigerate kiwifruit mixture until cold.

4. Pour ¼ cup kiwifruit mixture into each of 6 chilled bowls. Scoop ⅓ cup jalapeño ice milk in center of each bowl. Sprinkle raspberries evenly on top. Garnish with lime peel strips, if desired.

SOUTHWESTERN CHILI CHEESE EMPANADAS

Makes 32 appetizers

- ¾ **cup (3 ounces) finely shredded taco-flavored cheese***
- ⅓ **cup diced green chilies, drained**
- 1 **package (15 ounces) refrigerated pie crusts**
- 1 **egg**
  Chili powder

*If taco-flavored cheese is unavailable, toss ¾ cup shredded marbled Monterey Jack cheese with ½ teaspoon chili powder.

1. Combine cheese and chilies in small bowl.

2. Unfold 1 pastry crust on floured surface. Roll into 13-inch circle. Cut dough into 16 rounds using 3-inch cookie cutter, rerolling scraps as necessary. Repeat with remaining crust to total 32 circles.

3. Spoon 1 teaspoon cheese mixture in center of each dough round. Fold round in half, sealing edge with tines of fork.

4. Place empanadas on wax paper-lined baking sheets; freeze, uncovered, 1 hour or until firm. Place in resealable plastic food storage bags. Freeze up to 2 months, if desired.

5. To complete recipe, preheat oven to 400°F. Place frozen empanadas on ungreased baking sheet. Beat egg and 1 tablespoon water in small bowl; brush on empanadas. Sprinkle with chili powder.

6. Bake 12 to 17 minutes or until golden brown. Remove from baking sheet to wire rack to cool.

Make-Ahead Time: up to 2 months in freezer
Final Prep Time: 30 minutes

Serving Suggestion: Serve empanadas with salsa and sour cream.

SOUTHWESTERN CHILI CHEESE EMPANADAS

FAJITAS

Makes 5 servings

- ½ cup chopped onion
- ¼ cup GRANDMA'S® Molasses
- ¼ cup oil
- 2 tablespoons ROSE'S® Lime Juice
- 2 tablespoons chili powder
- ½ teaspoon oregano leaves
- 2 cloves garlic, minced
- 1 pound boneless top round or sirloin steak, cut into thin strips
- 10 flour tortillas (8 to 10 inches), warmed
- ½ cup (2 ounces) shredded Monterey Jack cheese
- 2 cups refried beans
- 2 tomatoes, chopped
- 1½ cups shredded lettuce
- 1 avocado, chopped
- 1 cup salsa
- Sour cream

1. In medium plastic bowl, combine onion, molasses, oil, lime juice, chili powder, oregano and garlic. Mix well. Add steak, stir to coat. Cover; marinate 4 to 6 hours or overnight, stirring occasionally.

2. In large skillet, stir-fry meat mixture 5 minutes or until brown. To serve, place meat in center of each tortilla; top with cheese, refried beans, tomatoes, lettuce, avocado and salsa. Fold up tortilla. Serve with sour cream.

CHIPOTLE CHILI CON CARNE

Makes 6 servings

1 tablespoon chili powder

1 tablespoon ground cumin

¾ pound beef for stew, cut into 1-inch pieces
   Nonstick cooking spray

1 can (about 14 ounces) reduced-sodium beef broth

1 tablespoon minced canned chipotle chilies in adobo
   sauce, or to taste

1 can (14½ ounces) diced tomatoes, undrained

1 large green bell pepper *or* 2 poblano chili peppers, cut into
   pieces

2 cans (16 ounces each) pinto or red beans, rinsed and
   drained
   Chopped fresh cilantro (optional)

1. Combine chili powder and cumin in medium bowl. Add beef and toss to coat. Spray large saucepan or Dutch oven with cooking spray; heat over medium heat. Add beef; cook 5 minutes, stirring occasionally. Add beef broth and chipotle chilies with sauce; bring to a boil. Reduce heat; cover and simmer 1 hour 15 minutes or until beef is very tender.

2. With slotted spoon, transfer beef to carving board, leaving juices in saucepan. Using two forks, shred beef. Return beef to saucepan; add tomatoes and bell pepper. Bring to a boil; stir in beans. Simmer, uncovered, 20 minutes or until bell pepper is tender. Garnish with cilantro, if desired.

Prep Time: 15 minutes
Cook Time: 1 hour 40 minutes

CHIPOTLE CHILI CON CARNE

FIESTA BEEF ENCHILADAS

Makes 4 servings

- 8 ounces 95% lean ground beef
- ½ cup sliced green onions
- 2 teaspoons minced garlic
- 1 cup cold cooked white or brown rice
- 1½ cups chopped tomato, divided
- ¾ cup frozen corn, thawed
- 1 cup (4 ounces) shredded reduced-fat Mexican cheese blend or Cheddar cheese, divided
- ½ cup salsa or picante sauce
- 12 (6- to 7-inch) corn tortillas
- 1 can (10 ounces) mild or hot enchilada sauce
- 1 cup shredded romaine lettuce

1. Preheat oven to 375°F. Spray 13×9-inch baking dish with nonstick cooking spray; set aside.

2. Cook ground beef in medium nonstick skillet over medium heat until no longer pink; drain. Add green onions and garlic; cook and stir 2 minutes.

3. Add rice, 1 cup tomato, corn, ½ cup cheese and salsa to meat mixture; mix well. Spoon mixture down center of tortillas. Roll up; place seam side down in prepared dish. Spoon enchilada sauce evenly over enchiladas.

4. Cover with foil; bake 20 minutes or until hot. Sprinkle with remaining ½ cup cheese; bake 5 minutes or until cheese melts. Top with lettuce and remaining ½ cup tomato.

Prep Time: 15 minutes
Cook Time: 35 minutes

Fiesta Beef Enchiladas

MILE-HIGH ENCHILADA PIE

Makes 4 to 6 servings

- 8 (6-inch) corn tortillas
- 1 jar (12 ounces) prepared salsa
- 1 can (15½ ounces) kidney beans, rinsed and drained
- 1 cup shredded cooked chicken
- 1 cup shredded Monterey Jack cheese with jalapeño peppers

SLOW COOKER DIRECTIONS

Prepare foil handles for slow cooker (see below); place in slow cooker. Place 1 tortilla on bottom of slow cooker. Top with small amount of salsa, beans, chicken and cheese. Continue layering using remaining ingredients, ending with cheese. Cover; cook on LOW 6 to 8 hours or on HIGH 3 to 4 hours. Pull out by foil handles. Garnish with cilantro and bell pepper, if desired.

Foil Handles: Tear off three 18×2-inch strips of heavy foil or use regular foil folded to double thickness. Crisscross foil strips in spoke design and place in slow cooker to make lifting of tortilla stack easier.

CINNAMON HONEY ICE CREAM

Makes 10 to 12 servings

- 2 cups milk
- ¾ cup honey
- 1 teaspoon cinnamon
  Pinch salt
- 2 eggs, beaten
- 2 cups heavy cream
- 2 teaspoons vanilla

1. Heat milk in large saucepan over medium heat but do not boil; stir in honey, cinnamon and salt.

2. Pour about ½ cup hot milk into eggs and beat with whisk; pour eggs into saucepan with remaining milk mixture. Cook and stir over medium-low heat 5 minutes (mixture should thicken slightly).

3. Cool to room temperature. Stir in cream and vanilla. Refrigerate overnight or until cold.

4. Freeze in ice cream maker according to manufacturer's directions.

MILE-HIGH ENCHILADA PIE

south-of-the-border
favorites

GREEN CHILI RICE

Makes 6 servings

- **1 cup uncooked white rice**
- **1 can (14½ ounces) fat-free reduced-sodium chicken broth plus water to measure 2 cups**
- **1 can (4 ounces) chopped mild green chilies**
- **½ medium yellow onion, peeled and diced**
- **1 teaspoon dried oregano leaves**
- **½ teaspoon salt (optional)**
- **½ teaspoon cumin seeds**
- **3 green onions, thinly sliced**
- **⅓ to ½ cup fresh cilantro leaves**

Combine rice, broth, chilies, yellow onion, oregano, salt, if desired, and cumin in large saucepan. Bring to a boil, uncovered, over high heat. Reduce heat to low; cover and simmer 18 minutes or until liquid is absorbed and rice is tender. Stir in green onions and cilantro. Garnish as desired.

GREEN CHILI RICE

TEQUILA-LIME PRAWNS

Makes 3 to 4 servings

- 1 **pound medium shrimp, peeled and deveined**
- 3 **tablespoons butter or margarine**
- 1 **tablespoon olive oil**
- 2 **large cloves garlic, minced**
- 2 **tablespoons tequila**
- 1 **tablespoon lime juice**
- ¼ **teaspoon salt**
- ¼ **teaspoon red pepper flakes**
- 3 **tablespoons coarsely chopped fresh cilantro**
  Hot cooked rice (optional)

Pat shrimp dry with paper towels. Heat butter and oil in large skillet over medium heat. When butter is melted, add garlic; cook 30 seconds. Add shrimp; cook 2 minutes, stirring occasionally. Stir in tequila, lime juice, salt and red pepper flakes. Cook 2 minutes or until most of liquid evaporates and shrimp are pink and glazed. Add cilantro; cook 10 seconds. Serve over hot cooked rice, if desired. Garnish with lime wedges, if desired.

CAMPBELL'S® BEEF & CHEDDAR SOFT TACOS

Makes 4 servings

- 1 **pound ground beef**
- 1 **can (10¾ ounces) CAMPBELL'S® Condensed Cheddar Cheese Soup**
- ½ **cup PACE® Chunky Salsa *or* Picante Sauce**
- 8 **flour tortillas (8-inch)**
- 2 **cups shredded lettuce (about ½ small head)**

1. In medium skillet over medium-high heat, cook beef until browned, stirring to separate meat. Pour off fat.

2. Add soup and salsa. Reduce heat to low and heat through.

3. Spoon *about ⅓ cup* meat mixture down center of each tortilla. Top with lettuce. Fold tortilla around filling. Serve with additional salsa.

Prep/Cook Time: 15 minutes

TEQUILA-LIME PRAWNS

SOPES

Makes about 35 appetizer servings

> 4 cups masa harina flour
> ½ cup vegetable shortening or lard
> 2½ cups warm water
> 1 can (7 ounces) ORTEGA® Diced Green Chiles
> 2 tablespoons vegetable oil, *divided*
> Toppings: warmed ORTEGA Refried Beans, shredded mild cheddar or shredded Monterey Jack cheese, ORTEGA Salsa (any flavor), sour cream, ORTEGA Pickled Jalapeños Slices

PLACE flour in large bowl; cut in vegetable shortening with pastry blender or two knives until mixture resembles coarse crumbs. Gradually add water, kneading until smooth. Add chiles; mix well. Form dough into 35 small balls. Pat each ball into 3-inch patty; place on waxed paper.

HEAT 1 teaspoon oil in large skillet over medium-high heat for 1 to 2 minutes. Cook patties for 3 minutes on each side or until golden brown, adding additional oil as needed.

TOP with beans, cheese, salsa, dollop of sour cream and jalapeños.

TACOS CON PUERCO

Makes 4 servings

> 1 pound ground pork
> 1 can (8 ounces) whole tomatoes, undrained, cut up
> ¼ cup chopped onion
> 1 tablespoon chili powder
> ¼ teaspoon garlic powder
> Salt and pepper
> 8 taco shells
> 2 fresh tomatoes, cut into wedges
> 2 cups shredded iceberg lettuce

In heavy skillet, brown ground pork; stir in undrained canned tomatoes, onion, chili powder and garlic powder. Bring to a boil; reduce heat and simmer, uncovered, until most liquid evaporates, about 15 minutes, stirring occasionally. Season to taste with salt and pepper. Heat taco shells according to package directions. Portion filling into shells; top with fresh tomatoes and lettuce.

*Favorite recipe from **National Pork Board***

BARBECUED CHICKEN WITH CHILI-ORANGE GLAZE

Makes 4 servings

- 1 to 2 dried de arbol chilies*
- ½ cup fresh orange juice
- 2 tablespoons tequila
- 2 cloves garlic, minced
- 1½ teaspoons grated orange peel
- ¼ teaspoon salt
- ¼ cup vegetable oil
- 1 broiler-fryer chicken (about 3 pounds), cut into quarters
  Orange slices (optional)
  Cilantro sprigs (optional)

For milder flavor, discard seeds from chili peppers. Chili peppers can sting and irritate the skin; wear rubber gloves when handling peppers and do not touch eyes. Wash hands after handling.

1. Crush chilies into coarse flakes in mortar with pestle. Combine chilies, orange juice, tequila, garlic, orange peel and salt in small bowl. Gradually add oil, whisking continuously, until marinade is thoroughly blended.

2. Arrange chicken in single layer in shallow glass baking dish. Pour marinade over chicken; turn pieces to coat. Marinate, covered, in refrigerator 2 to 3 hours, turning chicken and basting with marinade several times.

3. Prepare charcoal grill for direct cooking or preheat broiler. Drain chicken, reserving marinade. Bring marinade to a boil in small saucepan over high heat; boil 2 minutes. Grill chicken on covered grill or broil, 6 to 8 inches from heat, 15 minutes, brushing frequently with marinade. Turn chicken. Grill or broil 15 minutes more or until chicken is no longer pink in center and juices run clear, brushing frequently with marinade. *Do not baste during last 5 minutes of grilling.* Discard remaining marinade. Garnish with orange slices and cilantro, if desired.

BARBECUED CHICKEN WITH CHILI-ORANGE GLAZE

CRAB AND CORN ENCHILADA CASSEROLE

Makes 6 servings

> Spicy Tomato Sauce (recipe follows), divided
> 10 to 12 ounces fresh crabmeat or flaked surimi crab
> 1 package (10 ounces) frozen corn, thawed and drained
> 1½ cups (6 ounces) shredded Monterey Jack cheese, divided
> 1 can (4 ounces) diced mild green chilies
> 12 (6-inch) corn tortillas
> 1 lime, cut into 6 wedges
> Sour cream (optional)

1. Preheat oven to 350°F. Prepare Spicy Tomato Sauce.

2. Combine 2 cups Spicy Tomato Sauce, crabmeat, corn, 1 cup cheese and chilies in medium bowl. Cut each tortilla into 4 wedges. Place one-third of tortilla wedges in bottom of shallow 3- to 4-quart casserole, overlapping to make solid layer. Spread half of crab mixture on top. Repeat with another layer tortilla wedges, remaining crab mixture and remaining tortillas. Spread remaining 1 cup Spicy Tomato Sauce over top; cover.

3. Bake 30 to 40 minutes or until heated through. Sprinkle with remaining ½ cup cheese; bake uncovered 5 minutes or until cheese melts. Squeeze lime over individual servings. Serve with sour cream, if desired.

SPICY TOMATO SAUCE

Makes about 3 cups sauce

> 2 cans (15 ounces each) no-salt-added stewed tomatoes, undrained *or* 6 medium tomatoes
> 2 teaspoons olive oil
> 1 medium onion, chopped
> 1 tablespoon minced garlic
> 2 tablespoons chili powder
> 2 teaspoons ground cumin
> 2 teaspoons dried oregano leaves, crushed
> 1 teaspoon ground cinnamon
> ¼ teaspoon red pepper flakes
> ¼ teaspoon ground cloves

Place tomatoes with juice in food processor or blender; process until finely chopped. Set aside.

continued on page 30

CRAB AND CORN ENCHILADA CASSEROLE

Spicy Tomato Sauce, *continued*

Heat oil over medium-high heat in large saucepan or Dutch oven. Add onion and garlic. Cook and stir 5 minutes or until onion is tender. Add chili powder, cumin, oregano, cinnamon, pepper flakes and cloves. Cook and stir 1 minute. Add tomatoes; reduce heat to medium-low. Simmer, uncovered, 20 minutes or until sauce is reduced to 3 to 3¼ cups.

RED SNAPPER VERA CRUZ

Makes 4 servings

  4 **red snapper fillets (about 1 pound)**
  ¼ **cup fresh lime juice**
  1 **tablespoon fresh lemon juice**
  1 **teaspoon chili powder**
  4 **green onions with 4 inches of tops, sliced in ½-inch lengths**
  1 **tomato, coarsely chopped**
  ½ **cup chopped Anaheim or green bell pepper**
  ½ **cup chopped red bell pepper**
     Black pepper

1. Place red snapper in shallow 9- to 10-inch round microwavable baking dish. Combine lime juice, lemon juice and chili powder in small bowl. Pour over snapper. Marinate 10 minutes, turning once or twice.

2. Sprinkle green onions, tomato, Anaheim and red bell pepper over snapper. Season with black pepper. Cover dish loosely with vented plastic wrap. Microwave at HIGH 5 to 6 minutes or just until snapper flakes in center, rotating dish every 2 minutes. Let stand, covered, 4 minutes.

Prep and Cook Time: 22 minutes

RED SNAPPER VERA CRUZ

FESTIVE CHICKEN DIP

Makes 2 quarts dip (about 30 appetizers)

- 1½ **pounds boneless, skinless chicken breasts, finely chopped (about 3 cups)**
- ¼ **cup lime juice, divided**
- 2 **garlic cloves, minced**
- 1 **teaspoon salt**
- ½ **teaspoon ground black pepper**
- 1 **can (16 ounces) refried beans**
- 1½ **cups sour cream, divided**
- 1 **package (1¼ ounces) dry taco seasoning mix, divided**
- 1 **tablespoon picante sauce**
- 1 **avocado, chopped**
- 1 **tablespoon olive oil**
- 1 **cup (4 ounces) shredded sharp Cheddar cheese**
- 1 **small onion, finely chopped**
- 2 **tomatoes, finely chopped**
- 1 **can (2¼ ounces) sliced black olives, drained and chopped**
- 1 **bag (10 ounces) tortilla chips**
- **Fresh cilantro for garnish**

Place chicken in small bowl. Sprinkle with 3 tablespoons lime juice, garlic, salt and pepper; mix well. Set aside. Combine beans, ½ cup sour cream, 2½ tablespoons taco seasoning mix and picante sauce in medium bowl. Spread bean mixture in bottom of shallow 2-quart casserole dish. Combine avocado and remaining 1 tablespoon lime juice in small bowl; sprinkle over bean mixture. Combine remaining 1 cup sour cream and 2½ tablespoons taco seasoning mix in small bowl; set aside. Heat oil in large skillet over high heat until hot; add chicken in single layer. Do not stir. Cook about 2 minutes or until chicken is brown on bottom. Turn chicken and cook until other side is brown and no liquid remains. Break chicken into separate pieces with fork. Layer chicken, sour cream mixture, cheese, onion and tomatoes over avocado mixture. Top with olives. Refrigerate until completely chilled. Serve with chips. Garnish with cilantro.

*Favorite recipe from **National Chicken Council***

FESTIVE CHICKEN DIP

BEEF MOLE TAMALE PIE

Makes 6 servings

- 1½ pounds ground beef chuck
- 1 medium onion, chopped
- 1 green bell pepper, chopped
- 2 cloves garlic, minced
- 1 package (10 ounces) frozen whole kernel corn, partially thawed
- 1¼ cups medium-hot salsa
- 1 tablespoon unsweetened cocoa powder
- 2 teaspoons ground cumin
- 1½ teaspoons salt, divided
- 1 teaspoon dried oregano leaves
- ¼ teaspoon ground cinnamon
- 2 cups (8 ounces) shredded Monterey Jack or Cheddar cheese
- ⅓ cup chopped fresh cilantro
- 1 cup all-purpose flour
- ¾ cup yellow cornmeal
- 3 tablespoons sugar
- 2 teaspoons baking powder
- ⅔ cup milk
- 3 tablespoons butter, melted
- 1 egg, beaten
- Cilantro leaves, chili pepper and sour cream for garnish

1. Preheat oven to 400°F. Spray 11×7-inch baking dish with nonstick cooking spray. Brown beef with onion, bell pepper and garlic in large deep skillet or Dutch oven over medium heat. Pour off drippings. Stir in corn, salsa, cocoa, cumin, 1 teaspoon salt, oregano and cinnamon. Bring to a boil. Reduce heat to medium-low; simmer, uncovered, 8 minutes, stirring occasionally. Remove from heat; stir in cheese and cilantro. Spread in prepared dish.

2. Combine flour, cornmeal, sugar, baking powder and remaining ½ teaspoon salt in large bowl. Add milk, butter and egg; stir just until dry ingredients are moistened. Drop by spoonfuls evenly over meat mixture; spread batter evenly with spatula.

3. Bake 15 minutes. *Reduce oven temperature to 350°F.* Bake 20 minutes or until topping is light brown and filling is bubbly. Let stand 5 minutes before serving. Garnish, if desired.

Beef Mole Tamale Pie

CHICKEN FAJITAS

Makes 4 servings

4 boneless, skinless chicken breast halves
2 teaspoons ground cumin
1½ teaspoons TABASCO® brand Pepper Sauce
1 teaspoon chili powder
½ teaspoon salt
  Spicy Tomato Salsa (recipe follows)
  Corn Relish (page 38)
8 flour tortillas
1 tablespoon vegetable oil
3 large green onions, cut into 2-inch pieces
½ cup shredded Cheddar cheese
½ cup guacamole or sliced avocado
½ cup sour cream

Cut chicken breasts into ½-inch strips. In large bowl toss chicken strips with cumin, TABASCO® Sauce, chili powder and salt; set aside. Prepare Spicy Tomato Salsa and Corn Relish. Wrap tortillas in foil; heat in preheated 350°F oven 10 minutes or until warm. Meanwhile, in large skillet, heat vegetable oil over medium-high heat. Add chicken mixture; cook 4 minutes, stirring frequently. Add green onions; cook 1 minute longer or until chicken is browned and tender.

To serve, place chicken in center of each tortilla; add Salsa, Relish, cheese, guacamole and sour cream. Fold bottom quarter and both sides of tortilla to cover filling.

SPICY TOMATO SALSA

1 large ripe tomato, diced
1 tablespoon chopped cilantro
1 tablespoon lime juice
¼ teaspoon TABASCO® brand Pepper Sauce
¼ teaspoon salt

In medium bowl toss tomato, cilantro, lime juice, TABASCO® Sauce and salt.

continued on page 38

Chicken Fajitas

Chicken Fajitas, *continued*

CORN RELISH

    1 **can (11 ounces) corn, drained**
  ½ **cup diced green bell pepper**
    1 **tablespoon lime juice**
  ¼ **teaspoon TABASCO® brand Pepper Sauce**
  ¼ **teaspoon salt**

In medium bowl toss corn, green pepper, lime juice, TABASCO® Sauce and salt.

TORTILLA SOUP

Makes 6 servings

    1 **tablespoon butter or margarine**
  ½ **cup chopped green bell pepper**
  ½ **cup chopped onion**
  ½ **teaspoon ground cumin**
 3½ **cups (two 14½-ounce cans) chicken broth**
    1 **jar (16 ounces) ORTEGA® Salsa-Thick & Chunky**
    1 **cup whole-kernel corn**
    1 **tablespoon vegetable oil**
    6 **corn tortillas, cut into ½-inch strips**
  ¾ **cup (3 ounces) shredded 4 cheese Mexican blend**
      Sour cream (optional)

MELT butter in medium saucepan over medium heat. Add bell pepper, onion and cumin; cook for 3 to 4 minutes or until tender. Stir in broth, salsa and corn. Bring to a boil. Reduce heat to low; cook for 5 minutes.

HEAT vegetable oil in medium skillet over medium-high heat. Add tortilla strips; cook for 3 to 4 minutes or until tender.

SERVE in soup bowls. Top with tortilla strips, cheese and a dollop of sour cream.

TORTILLA SOUP

SPICY PORK QUESADILLAS

Makes 16 servings

- ½ **pound lean ground pork**
- ¼ **cup diced onion**
- 1 **clove garlic, minced**
- ¼ **cup chopped fresh cilantro leaves**
- ¼ **teaspoon ground cumin**
- ¼ **teaspoon dried oregano leaves, crushed**
- ½ **jalapeño pepper,* minced**
- 4 **(10-inch) flour tortillas**
- 4 **tablespoons shredded Cheddar or Monterey Jack cheese**

*Jalapeño peppers can sting and irritate the skin; wear rubber gloves when handling peppers and do not touch eyes. Wash hands after handling.

In large nonstick skillet over medium-high heat, cook pork, onion and garlic until browned; drain off any drippings and remove to large bowl. Stir cilantro, cumin, oregano and jalapeño into pork mixture. Wipe out skillet with paper towel and heat over medium-high heat. Place 1 tortilla in skillet; top with half the pork mixture, spreading evenly. Sprinkle with 2 tablespoons cheese. Top with another tortilla and cook 2 to 3 minutes or until browned, pressing down occasionally on top tortilla. Turn and brown other side; remove to cutting board and cut into 8 wedges. Repeat with remaining ingredients to make 8 more quesadilla wedges. Serve with salsa, if desired.

Prep Time: 20 minutes

*Favorite recipe from **National Pork Board***

HOT CHEESY CHILI DIP

Makes about 5 cups

- 1 **pound lean ground beef**
- ½ **cup chopped onion**
- 1 **package (1 pound) pasteurized process cheese spread with jalapeño pepper, cut into cubes**
- 1 **can (15 ounces) kidney beans, drained**
- 1 **bottle (12 ounces) HEINZ® Chili Sauce**
- ¼ **cup chopped fresh parsley**
  Tortilla chips or crackers

In large saucepan, cook beef and onion until onion is tender; drain. Stir in cheese, beans and chili sauce; heat, stirring until cheese is melted. Stir in parsley. Serve warm with tortilla chips or crackers.

CAMPBELL'S® COD VERA CRUZ

Makes 4 servings

- 1 **pound fresh *or* thawed frozen cod *or* haddock fillets**
- 1 **can (10¾ ounces) CAMPBELL'S® Condensed Tomato Soup**
- 1 **can (10½ ounces) CAMPBELL'S® Condensed Chicken Broth**
- ⅓ **cup PACE® Chunky Salsa *or* Picante Sauce**
- 1 **tablespoon lime juice**
- 2 **teaspoons chopped fresh cilantro**
- 1 **teaspoon dried oregano leaves, crushed**
- ⅛ **teaspoon garlic powder *or* 1 clove garlic, minced**
- 4 **cups hot cooked rice**

1. Place fish in 2-quart shallow baking dish.

2. Mix soup, broth, salsa, lime juice, cilantro, oregano and garlic powder. Pour over fish. Bake at 400°F. for 20 minutes or until fish flakes easily when tested with a fork. Serve over rice.

Prep Time: 10 minutes
Cook Time: 20 minutes

mexican food made easy

TURKEY AND BEAN TOSTADAS

Makes 6 servings

- 6 (8-inch) flour tortillas
- 1 pound 93% lean ground turkey
- 1 can (15 ounces) chili beans in chili sauce
- ½ teaspoon chili powder
- 3 cups washed and shredded romaine lettuce
- 1 large tomato, chopped
- ¼ cup chopped fresh cilantro
- ¼ cup (1 ounce) shredded reduced-fat Monterey Jack cheese
- ½ cup reduced-fat sour cream (optional)

1. Preheat oven to 350°F. Place tortillas on baking sheets. Bake 7 minutes or until crisp. Place on individual plates.

2. Heat large nonstick skillet over medium-high heat until hot. Add turkey. Cook and stir until turkey is browned; drain. Add beans and chili powder. Cook 5 minutes over medium heat. Divide turkey mixture evenly among tortillas. Top with remaining ingredients and sour cream, if desired.

Prep and Cook Time: 20 minutes

TURKEY AND BEAN TOSTADAS

BEAN AND VEGETABLE BURRITOS

Makes 4 servings

1 tablespoon olive oil

1 medium onion, thinly sliced

1 jalapeño pepper,* seeded and minced

1 tablespoon chili powder

3 cloves garlic, minced

2 teaspoons dried oregano leaves

1 teaspoon ground cumin

1 large sweet potato, baked, cooled, peeled and diced *or*
 1 can (16 ounces) yams in syrup, rinsed, drained and diced

1 can (about 15 ounces) black beans or pinto beans, rinsed and drained

1 cup frozen corn, thawed and drained

1 green bell pepper, chopped

2 tablespoons lime juice

¾ cup (3 ounces) shredded reduced-fat Monterey Jack cheese

4 (10-inch) flour tortillas

Sour cream (optional)

*Jalapeño peppers can sting and irritate the skin; wear rubber gloves when handling peppers and do not touch eyes. Wash hands after handling.

1. Preheat oven to 350°F. Heat oil in large saucepan or Dutch oven over medium-high heat. Add onion and cook, stirring often, 10 minutes or until golden. Add jalapeño pepper, chili powder, garlic, oregano and cumin; stir 1 minute more. Add 1 tablespoon water and stir; remove from heat. Stir in sweet potato, beans, corn, bell pepper and lime juice.

2. Spoon 2 tablespoons cheese in center of each tortilla. Top with 1 cup filling. Fold all 4 sides around filling to enclose. Place burritos seam side down on baking sheet. Cover with foil and bake 30 minutes or until heated through. Serve with sour cream, if desired.

BEAN AND VEGETABLE BURRITO

NACHO SALAD

Makes 4 servings

- 3 ounces (about 60) GUILTLESS GOURMET® Unsalted Baked Tortilla Chips
- 2 teaspoons water
- ½ cup GUILTLESS GOURMET® Black Bean Dip (Spicy or Mild)
- 4 cups shredded romaine lettuce
- 2 medium tomatoes (red or yellow), chopped
- ½ cup (2 ounces) grated Cheddar cheese
- ½ cup GUILTLESS GOURMET® Salsa (Roasted Red Pepper or Southwestern Grill)

Divide and spread tortilla chips among 4 plates. Stir water into bean dip in small microwave-safe bowl or small saucepan. Microwave bean dip on HIGH (100% power) 2 to 3 minutes or heat over medium heat until warm. Evenly drizzle heated dip over tortilla chips. Sprinkle lettuce, tomatoes and cheese evenly over tortilla chips. To serve, spoon 2 tablespoons tomatillo salsa over each salad.

OLD-FASHIONED CORN RELISH

Makes about 3 cups

- ⅓ cup cider vinegar
- 2 tablespoons sugar
- 1 tablespoon cornstarch
- 3 tablespoons *French's*® Classic Yellow® Mustard
- ¼ teaspoon seasoned salt
- 1 package (9 ounces) frozen corn, thawed and drained
- ½ cup chopped celery
- ½ cup chopped red bell pepper
- ¼ cup finely chopped red onion
- 3 tablespoons sweet pickle relish

Combine vinegar, sugar and cornstarch in large microwave-safe bowl; mix well. Stir in mustard and salt. Microwave, uncovered, on HIGH 1 to 2 minutes or until thickened, stirring once. Add corn, celery, pepper, onion and pickle relish; toss well to coat evenly. Cover and refrigerate 30 minutes before serving. Serve as a relish on hamburgers or hot dogs, or serve on the side with grilled meats.

Prep Time: 10 minutes
Cook Time: 2 minutes
Chill Time: 30 minutes

Nacho Salad

FAJITAS WITH AVOCADO SALSA

Makes 4 servings

- 1 beef flank steak (1¼ to 1½ pounds)
- ¼ cup tequila or nonalcoholic beer
- 3 tablespoons fresh lime juice
- 1 tablespoon seeded and minced jalapeño pepper*
- 2 large cloves garlic, minced
  Avocado Salsa (recipe follows)
- 8 (6- or 7-inch) flour tortillas
- 1 large red bell pepper, cut into 4 vertical strips
- 1 large green bell pepper, cut into 4 vertical strips
- 4 slices red onion, cut ¼ inch thick

Jalapeño peppers can sting and irritate the skin; wear rubber gloves when handling peppers and do not touch eyes. Wash hands after handling.

1. Place steak in large resealable plastic food storage bag. Combine tequila, lime juice, jalapeño and garlic in small bowl; pour over steak. Seal bag tightly; turn to coat. Marinate in refrigerator 1 to 4 hours, turning once.

2. Prepare grill for direct cooking.

3. Meanwhile, prepare Avocado Salsa. Wrap tortillas in heavy-duty foil.

4. Drain steak; discard marinade. Place steak, bell peppers and onion slices on grid over medium heat. Grill, uncovered, 17 to 21 minutes or until desired doneness, turning steak, bell peppers and onions halfway through grilling time. Place tortilla packet on grid during last 5 to 7 minutes of grilling; turn halfway through grilling time to heat through.

5. Transfer steak to carving board. Carve steak across the grain into thin slices. Slice bell peppers into thin strips. Separate onion slices into rings. Divide among tortillas; roll up and top with Avocado Salsa.

AVOCADO SALSA

Makes about 1½ cups

- 1 large ripe avocado, coarsely chopped
- 1 large tomato, seeded and diced
- 3 tablespoons chopped fresh cilantro
- 1 tablespoon vegetable oil
- 1 tablespoon fresh lime juice
- 2 teaspoons seeded and minced jalapeño pepper*
- 1 clove garlic, minced
- ½ teaspoon salt

Jalapeño peppers can sting and irritate the skin; wear rubber gloves when handling peppers and do not touch eyes. Wash hands after handling.

continued on page 50

FAJITAS WITH AVOCADO SALSA

Fajitas with Avocado Salsa, *continued*

1. Place avocado in medium bowl.

2. Gently stir in tomato, cilantro, oil, lime juice, jalapeño, garlic and salt until well combined. Let stand at room temperature while grilling steak. Cover; refrigerate if preparing in advance. Bring to room temperature before serving.

SPEEDY BEEF & BEAN BURRITOS

Makes 4 servings

> 8 (7-inch) flour tortillas
> 1 pound ground beef
> 1 cup chopped onion
> 1 teaspoon minced garlic
> 1 can (15 ounces) black beans, drained and rinsed
> 1 cup spicy, thick and chunky salsa
> 2 teaspoons ground cumin
> ¼ cup chopped cilantro
> 2 cups (8 ounces) shredded cojack or Monterey Jack cheese

1. Wrap tortillas in foil; place on center rack in oven. Heat oven to 350°F; heat tortillas 15 minutes.

2. While tortillas are warming, prepare burrito filling. Combine beef, onion and garlic in large skillet; cook over medium-high heat until beef is no longer pink, breaking beef apart with wooden spoon. Pour off drippings.

3. Stir beans, salsa and cumin into beef mixture; reduce heat to medium. Cover and simmer 10 minutes, stirring once.

4. Stir cilantro into filling. Spoon filling down centers of warm tortillas; top with cheese. Roll up and serve immediately.

Prep and Cook Time: 20 minutes

Speedy Beef & Bean Burritos

GUADALAJARA BEEF AND SALSA

Makes 4 servings

1 **bottle (12 ounces) Mexican dark beer***
¼ **cup soy sauce**
2 **cloves garlic, minced**
1 **teaspoon ground cumin**
1 **teaspoon chili powder**
1 **teaspoon hot pepper sauce**
4 **boneless beef sirloin or top loin strip steaks (4 to 6 ounces each)**
Salt and black pepper
Red, green and yellow bell peppers, cut lengthwise into quarters, seeded (optional)
Salsa (recipe follows)
Flour tortillas (optional)
Lime wedges

Substitute any beer for Mexican dark beer.

Combine beer, soy sauce, garlic, cumin, chili powder and hot pepper sauce in large shallow glass dish or large heavy plastic food storage bag. Add beef; cover dish or close bag. Marinate in refrigerator up to 12 hours, turning beef several times. Remove beef from marinade; discard marinade. Season with salt and black pepper.

Oil hot grid to help prevent sticking. Grill beef and bell peppers, if desired, on covered grill, over medium KINGSFORD® Briquets, 8 to 12 minutes, turning once. Beef should be of medium doneness and peppers should be tender. Serve with salsa, tortillas, if desired, and lime wedges.

SALSA

Makes about 2 cups

2 **cups coarsely chopped seeded tomatoes**
2 **green onions with tops, sliced**
1 **clove garlic, minced**
1 **to 2 teaspoons minced seeded jalapeño or serrano chili pepper, fresh or canned**
1 **tablespoon olive or vegetable oil**
2 **to 3 teaspoons lime juice**
8 **to 10 sprigs fresh cilantro, minced (optional)**
½ **teaspoon salt or to taste**
½ **teaspoon sugar or to taste**
¼ **teaspoon black pepper**

continued on page 54

GUADALAJARA BEEF AND SALSA

Guadalajara Beef and Salsa, *continued*

Combine tomatoes, green onions, garlic, chili pepper, oil and lime juice in medium bowl. Stir in cilantro, if desired. Season with salt, sugar and black pepper. Adjust seasonings to taste, adding lime juice or chili pepper, if desired.

SEÑOR NACHO DIP

Makes 4 servings

> 4 ounces fat-free cream cheese
> ½ cup (2 ounces) reduced-fat Cheddar cheese
> ¼ cup mild or medium chunky salsa
> 2 teaspoons low-fat (2%) milk
> 4 ounces baked tortilla chips or assorted fresh vegetable dippers

1. Combine cream cheese and Cheddar cheese in small saucepan; stir over low heat until melted. Stir in salsa and milk; heat thoroughly, stirring occasionally.

2. Transfer dip to small serving bowl. Serve with tortilla chips. Garnish with hot peppers and cilantro, if desired.

Olé Dip: Substitute reduced-fat Monterey Jack cheese or taco cheese for Cheddar cheese.

Spicy Mustard Dip: Omit tortilla chips. Substitute 2 teaspoons spicy brown or honey mustard for salsa. Serve with fresh vegetable dippers or pretzels.

CAMPBELL'S® E-Z CHICKEN TORTILLA BAKE

Makes 4 servings

> 1 can (10¾ ounces) CAMPBELL'S® Condensed Tomato Soup
> 1 cup PACE® Chunky Salsa *or* Picante Sauce
> ½ cup milk
> 2 cups cubed cooked chicken *or* turkey
> 8 corn tortillas (6- or 8-inch), cut into 1-inch pieces
> 1 cup shredded Cheddar cheese (4 ounces)

1. In 2-quart shallow baking dish mix soup, salsa, milk, chicken, tortillas and **half** the cheese. **Cover.**

2. Bake at 400°F. for 30 minutes or until hot. Top with remaining cheese.

Prep Time: 10 minutes
Cook Time: 30 minutes

Señor Nacho Dip

BAJA FISH TACOS

Makes 6 servings

- ½ **cup sour cream**
- ½ **cup mayonnaise**
- ¼ **cup chopped fresh cilantro**
- 1 **package (1.25 ounces) ORTEGA® Taco Seasoning Mix,** *divided*
- 1 **pound (about 4) cod or other white fish fillets, cut into 1-inch pieces**
- 2 **tablespoons vegetable oil**
- 2 **tablespoons lemon juice**
- 1 **package (12) ORTEGA® Taco Shells**

TOPPINGS

Shredded cabbage, chopped tomato, lime juice, ORTEGA® Thick & Smooth Taco Sauce

COMBINE sour cream, mayonnaise, cilantro and *2 tablespoons* taco seasoning mix in small bowl.

COMBINE cod, vegetable oil, lemon juice and *remaining* taco seasoning mix in medium bowl; pour into large skillet. Cook, stirring constantly, over medium-high heat for 4 to 5 minutes or until fish flakes easily when tested with fork.

FILL taco shells with fish mixture. Layer with desired toppings. Top with sour cream sauce.

Tip: Try a variety of fish and seafood such as shark, shrimp, crab or lobster in these fresh-tasting tacos.

BAJA FISH TACOS

STACKED BURRITO PIE

Makes 4 servings

- ½ cup **GUILTLESS GOURMET**® Mild Black Bean Dip
- 2 teaspoons water
- 5 low-fat flour tortillas (6 inches each)
- ½ cup nonfat sour cream or plain yogurt
- ½ cup **GUILTLESS GOURMET**® Roasted Red Pepper Salsa
- 1¼ cups (5 ounces) shredded low-fat Monterey Jack cheese
- 4 cups shredded iceberg or romaine lettuce
- ½ cup **GUILTLESS GOURMET**® Salsa (Roasted Red Pepper or Southwestern Grill)
- Lime slices and chili pepper (optional)

Preheat oven to 350°F. Combine bean dip and 2 teaspoons water in small bowl; mix well. Line 7½-inch springform pan with 1 tortilla. Spread 2 tablespoons bean dip mixture over tortilla, then spread with 2 tablespoons sour cream and 2 tablespoons red pepper salsa. Sprinkle with ¼ cup cheese. Repeat layers 3 more times. Place remaining tortilla on top and sprinkle with remaining ¼ cup cheese.

Bake 40 minutes or until heated through. (Place sheet of foil under springform pan to catch any juices that may seep through the bottom.) Cool slightly before unmolding. To serve, cut into 4 quarters. Place 1 cup lettuce on each of 4 serving plates. Top lettuce with 1 quarter burrito pie and 2 tablespoons salsa. Garnish with lime slices and pepper, if desired.

STACKED BURRITO PIE

CORN & BEAN SALSA

Makes 6 servings (about 4 cups salsa)

- ⅓ cup olive oil
- 3 tablespoons *Frank's® RedHot®* Original Cayenne Pepper Sauce
- 3 tablespoons red wine vinegar
- 2 tablespoons minced fresh cilantro leaves
- 1 clove garlic, minced
- ½ teaspoon chili powder
- ¼ teaspoon salt
- 1 package (9 ounces) frozen corn, thawed and drained
- 1 can (16 ounces) black beans, drained and rinsed
- 1 large ripe tomato, chopped
- 2 green onions, thinly sliced

Whisk together oil, **Frank's RedHot** Sauce, vinegar, cilantro, garlic, chili powder and salt in large bowl until blended. Add corn, beans, tomato and onions; toss well to coat evenly. Cover and refrigerate 30 minutes before serving. Serve with grilled steak or hamburgers.

Prep Time: 15 minutes
Chill Time: 30 minutes

TOP TO BOTTOM: CORN & BEAN SALSA, OLD-FASHIONED CORN RELISH
(PAGE 46)

61

mexican food made easy

CAMPBELL'S® 5-MINUTE BURRITO WRAPS

Makes 6 burritos

> 1 can (11¼ ounces) CAMPBELL'S® Condensed Fiesta Chili Beef Soup
> 6 flour tortillas (8-inch)
> Shredded Cheddar cheese

MICROWAVE DIRECTIONS

1. Spoon 2 tablespoons soup down center of each tortilla. Top with cheese. Fold tortilla around filling.

2. Place seam-side down on microwave-safe plate and microwave on HIGH 2 minutes or until hot.

Prep/Cook Time: 5 minutes

CAMPBELL'S® CHEESY PICANTE POTATOES

Makes 6 to 8 servings

> 1 can (10¾ ounces) CAMPBELL'S® Condensed Cheddar Cheese Soup
> ½ cup PACE® Picante Sauce *or* Chunky Salsa
> 1 teaspoon garlic powder
> 4 cups cubed cooked potatoes (about 4 medium)
> Paprika
> 2 tablespoons chopped fresh cilantro

In medium skillet mix soup, picante sauce and garlic powder. Add potatoes. Over medium heat, heat through, stirring often. Sprinkle with paprika and cilantro. Serve with additional picante sauce.

Prep Time: 10 minutes
Cook Time: 10 minutes

wake up with a mexican breakfast

Eggs Santa Fe

Makes 2 servings

- **2 eggs**
- **½ cup GUILTLESS GOURMET® Black Bean Dip (Spicy or Mild)**
- **¼ cup GUILTLESS GOURMET® Southwestern Grill Salsa**
- **1 ounce (about 20) GUILTLESS GOURMET® Unsalted Baked Tortilla Chips**
- **2 tablespoons low fat sour cream**
- **1 teaspoon chopped fresh cilantro**
- **Fresh cilantro sprigs (optional)**

To poach eggs, bring water to a boil in small skillet over high heat; reduce heat to medium-low and maintain a simmer. Gently break eggs into water, being careful not to break yolks. Cover and simmer 5 minutes or until desired firmness.

Meanwhile, place bean dip in small microwave-safe bowl or small saucepan. Microwave bean dip on HIGH (100% power) 2 to 3 minutes or heat over medium heat until warm. To serve, spread ¼ cup warm bean dip in center of serving plate; top with 1 poached egg and 2 tablespoons salsa. Arrange 10 tortilla chips around egg. Dollop with 1 tablespoon sour cream and sprinkle with ½ teaspoon chopped cilantro. Repeat with remaining ingredients. Garnish with cilantro sprigs, if desired.

EGG SANTA FE

BLACK BEAN PANCAKES & SALSA

Makes 4 servings

- 1 cup GUILTLESS GOURMET® Black Bean Dip (Spicy or Mild)
- 2 egg whites
- ½ cup unbleached all-purpose flour
- ½ cup skim milk
- 1 tablespoon canola oil
  Nonstick cooking spray
- ½ cup fat free sour cream
- ½ cup GUILTLESS GOURMET® Roasted Red Pepper Salsa
  Yellow tomatoes and fresh mint leaves (optional)

For pancake batter, place bean dip, egg whites, flour, milk and oil in blender or food processor; blend until smooth. Refrigerate 2 hours or overnight.

Preheat oven to 350°F. Coat large nonstick skillet with cooking spray; heat over medium heat until hot. For each pancake, spoon 2 tablespoons batter into skillet; cook until bubbles form and break on pancake surface. Turn pancakes over; cook until lightly browned on other side. Place on baking sheet; keep warm in oven. Repeat to make 16 small pancakes. (If batter becomes too thick, thin with more milk.) Serve hot with sour cream and salsa. Garnish with tomatoes and mint, if desired.

BLACK BEAN PANCAKES & SALSA

SCRAMBLED EGG BURRITOS

Makes 4 servings

    Nonstick cooking spray
- **1 red bell pepper, chopped**
- **5 green onions, sliced**
- **½ teaspoon red pepper flakes**
- **1 cup cholesterol-free egg substitute *or* 8 egg whites**
- **1 tablespoon chopped fresh cilantro or parsley**
- **4 (8-inch) flour tortillas**
- **½ cup (2 ounces) shredded Monterey Jack cheese**
- **⅓ cup salsa**

1. Spray medium nonstick skillet with cooking spray. Heat over medium heat until hot. Add bell pepper, onions and pepper flakes. Cook and stir 3 minutes or until vegetables are crisp-tender.

2. Add egg substitute to vegetables. Reduce heat to low. Cook and stir 3 minutes or until set. Sprinkle with cilantro.

3. Stack tortillas and wrap in paper towels. Microwave at HIGH 1 minute or until tortillas are hot.

4. Place ¼ egg mixture on each tortilla. Sprinkle with 2 tablespoons cheese. Fold sides over to enclose filling. Serve with salsa.

PACE® BREAKFAST TACOS

Makes 4 tacos

- **1 tablespoon margarine *or* butter**
- **1 medium potato, cooked and diced (about 1 cup)**
- **4 eggs, beaten**
- **4 slices bacon, cooked and crumbled**
- **4 flour tortillas (8-inch)**
- **¾ cup shredded Cheddar cheese (3 ounces)**
- **½ cup PACE® Picante Sauce *or* Chunky Salsa**

1. In medium skillet over medium heat, heat margarine. Add potato and cook until lightly browned. Add eggs and bacon and cook until eggs are set but still moist.

2. Warm tortillas according to package directions. Spoon about *½ cup* potato mixture down center of each tortilla. Top with cheese and picante sauce. Roll up.

Prep Time: 15 minutes
Cook Time: 10 minutes

SCRAMBLED EGG BURRITO

SPICY MEXICAN FRITTATA

Makes 4 servings

- 1 fresh jalapeño pepper*
- 1 clove garlic
- 1 medium tomato, peeled, halved, seeded and quartered
- ½ teaspoon ground coriander
- ½ teaspoon chili powder
    Nonstick cooking spray
- ½ cup chopped onion
- 1 cup frozen corn
- 6 egg whites
- 2 eggs
- ¼ cup fat-free (skim) milk
- ¼ teaspoon salt
- ¼ teaspoon black pepper
- ¼ cup (1 ounce) shredded part-skim farmer or mozzarella cheese

Jalapeño peppers can sting and irritate the skin; wear rubber gloves when handling peppers and do not touch eyes. Wash hands after handling.

1. Add jalapeño pepper and garlic to food processor or blender. Process until finely chopped. Add tomato, coriander and chili powder. Cover; process until tomato is almost smooth.

2. Spray large skillet with cooking spray; heat over medium heat until hot. Cook and stir onion until tender. Stir in tomato mixture and corn. Cook 3 to 4 minutes or until liquid is almost evaporated, stirring occasionally.

3. Combine egg whites, eggs, milk, salt and black pepper in medium bowl. Add egg mixture all at once to skillet. Cook, without stirring, 2 minutes or until eggs begin to set. Run large spoon around edge of skillet, lifting eggs for even cooking. Remove skillet from heat when eggs are almost set but surface is still moist.

4. Sprinkle with cheese. Cover; let stand 3 to 4 minutes or until surface is set and cheese is melted. Cut into 4 wedges.

SPICY MEXICAN FRITTATA

HAM AND EGG ENCHILADAS

Makes 4 servings

    2 tablespoons butter or margarine
    1 small red bell pepper, chopped
    3 green onions with tops, sliced
    ½ cup diced ham
    8 eggs
    8 (7- to 8-inch) flour tortillas
    2 cups (8 ounces) shredded Colby-Jack cheese or
        Pepper-Jack cheese, divided
    1 can (10 ounces) enchilada sauce
    ½ cup prepared salsa
      Sliced avocado, fresh cilantro and red pepper slices for
        garnish

1. Preheat oven to 350°F.

2. Melt butter in large nonstick skillet over medium heat. Add bell pepper and onions; cook and stir 2 minutes. Add ham; cook and stir 1 minute.

3. Lightly beat eggs with wire whisk in medium bowl. Add eggs to skillet; cook until eggs are set but still soft, stirring occasionally.

4. Spoon about ⅓ cup egg mixture evenly down center of each tortilla; top with 1 tablespoon cheese. Roll tortillas up and place seam side down in shallow 11×7-inch baking dish.

5. Combine enchilada sauce and salsa in small bowl; pour evenly over enchiladas.

6. Cover enchiladas with foil; bake 20 minutes. Uncover; sprinkle with remaining cheese. Continue baking 10 minutes or until enchiladas are hot and cheese is melted. Garnish, if desired. Serve immediately.

HAM AND EGG ENCHILADAS

desserts & drinks
fit for a fiesta

RICE PUDDING MEXICANA

Makes 6 servings

- **1 package instant rice pudding**
- **1 tablespoon vanilla**
- **¼ teaspoon ground cinnamon**
- **Dash ground cloves**
- **¼ cup slivered almonds**
- **Additional ground cinnamon**

1. Prepare rice pudding according to package directions.

2. Remove pudding from heat; stir in vanilla, ¼ teaspoon cinnamon and cloves. Pour evenly into 6 individual dessert dishes.

3. Sprinkle evenly with almonds and additional cinnamon. Serve warm.

Prep and Cook Time: 18 minutes

Rice Pudding Mexicana

SPANISH CHURROS

Makes about 3 dozen cookies

- **1 cup water**
- **¼ cup (½ stick) butter**
- **6 tablespoons sugar, divided**
- **¼ teaspoon salt**
- **1 cup all-purpose flour**
- **2 eggs**
- **Vegetable oil for frying**
- **1 teaspoon ground cinnamon**

1. Place water, butter, 2 tablespoons sugar and salt in medium saucepan; bring to a boil over high heat. Remove from heat; add flour. Beat with spoon until dough forms ball and releases from side of pan. Vigorously beat in eggs, 1 at a time, until mixture is smooth. Spoon dough into pastry bag fitted with large star tip. Pipe 3×1-inch strips onto waxed-paper-lined baking sheet. Freeze 20 minutes.

2. Pour vegetable oil into 10-inch skillet to ¾-inch depth. Heat oil to 375°F. Transfer frozen dough to hot oil with large spatula. Fry 4 or 5 cookies at a time until deep golden brown, 3 to 4 minutes, turning once. Remove cookies with slotted spoon to paper towels; drain.

3. Combine remaining 4 tablespoons sugar with cinnamon. Place in paper bag. Add warm cookies, 1 at a time; close bag and shake until cookie is coated with sugar mixture. Remove to wire rack. Repeat with remaining sugar mixture and cookies; cool completely. Store tightly covered at room temperature or freeze up to 3 months.

SPANISH CHURROS

CARAMEL FLAN

Makes 6 to 8 servings

- 1 **cup sugar, divided**
- 2 **cups half-and-half**
- 1 **cup milk**
- 1½ **teaspoons vanilla**
- 6 **eggs**
- 2 **egg yolks**
  Hot water
  Fresh whole and sliced strawberries for garnish

1. Preheat oven to 325°F. Heat 5½- to 6-cup ring mold in oven 10 minutes or until hot.

2. Heat ½ cup sugar in heavy, medium skillet over medium-high heat 5 to 8 minutes or until sugar is completely melted and deep amber color, stirring frequently. *Do not allow sugar to burn.*

3. Immediately pour caramelized sugar into ring mold. Holding mold with potholder, quickly rotate to coat bottom and sides evenly with sugar. Place mold on wire rack. *Caution: Caramelized sugar is very hot; do not touch it.*

4. Combine half-and-half and milk in heavy 2-quart saucepan. Heat over medium heat until almost simmering; remove from heat. Add remaining ½ cup sugar and vanilla, stirring until sugar is dissolved.

5. Lightly beat eggs and egg yolks in large bowl until blended but not foamy; gradually stir in milk mixture. Pour custard into ring mold.

6. Place mold in large baking pan; pour hot water into baking pan to depth of ½ inch. Bake 35 to 40 minutes until knife inserted into center of custard comes out clean.

7. Remove mold from water bath; place on wire rack. Let stand 30 minutes. Cover and refrigerate 1½ to 2 hours until thoroughly chilled.

8. To serve, loosen inner and outer edges of flan with tip of small knife. Cover mold with rimmed serving plate; invert and lift off mold. Garnish with strawberries, if desired. Spoon some of the melted caramel over each serving.

CARAMEL FLAN

MEXICAN CHOCOLATE MACAROONS

Makes 3 dozen cookies

> 1 package (8 ounces) semisweet baking chocolate, divided
> 1¾ cups plus ⅓ cup whole almonds, divided
> ¾ cup sugar
> 1 teaspoon ground cinnamon
> 1 teaspoon vanilla
> 2 egg whites

1. Preheat oven to 400°F. Grease cookie sheets; set aside.

2. Place 5 squares chocolate in food processor; process until coarsely chopped. Add 1¾ cups almonds and sugar; process using on/off pulsing action until mixture is finely ground. Add cinnamon, vanilla and egg whites; process just until mixture forms moist dough.

3. Form dough into 1-inch balls (dough will be sticky). Place 2 inches apart on prepared baking sheets. Press 1 almond on top of each cookie.

4. Bake 8 to 10 minutes or just until set. Cool 2 minutes on cookie sheets. Remove cookies to wire racks. Cool completely.

5. Heat remaining 3 squares chocolate in small saucepan over very low heat until melted. Spoon chocolate into small resealable plastic food storage bag. Cut small corner off bottom of bag with scissors. Drizzle chocolate over cookies. Let stand until set.

Prep and Bake Time: 30 minutes

MEXICAN CHOCOLATE MACAROONS

TOASTED ALMOND HORCHATA

Makes 8 to 10 servings

3½ cups water, divided
2 (3-inch) cinnamon sticks
1 cup uncooked instant white rice
1 cup slivered almonds, toasted
3 cups cold water
¾ to 1 cup sugar
½ teaspoon vanilla
Lime wedges for garnish

1. Combine 3 cups water and cinnamon sticks in medium saucepan. Cover and bring to a boil over high heat. Reduce heat to medium-low. Simmer 15 minutes. Remove from heat; let cool to temperature of hot tap water. Measure cinnamon water to equal 3 cups, adding additional hot water if needed.

2. Place rice in food processor; process using on/off pulsing action 1 to 2 minutes or until rice is powdery. Add almonds; process until finely ground (mixture will begin to stick together). Remove rice mixture to medium bowl; stir in cinnamon water and cinnamon sticks. Let stand 1 hour or until mixture is thick and rice grains are soft.

3. Remove cinnamon sticks; discard. Pour mixture into food processor. Add remaining ½ cup water; process 2 to 4 minutes or until mixture is very creamy. Strain mixture through fine-meshed sieve or several layers of dampened cheesecloth into half-gallon pitcher. Stir in 3 cups cold water, sugar and vanilla; stir until sugar is completely dissolved.

4. To serve, pour over ice cubes, if desired. Garnish with lime wedges, if desired.

TOASTED ALMOND HORCHATA

MEXICAN WEDDING COOKIES

Makes about 4 dozen cookies

- **1 cup pecan pieces or halves**
- **1 cup (2 sticks) butter, softened**
- **2 cups powdered sugar, divided**
- **2 cups all-purpose flour, divided**
- **2 teaspoons vanilla**
- **⅛ teaspoon salt**

1. Place pecans in food processor. Process using on/off pulsing action until pecans are ground but not pasty.

2. Beat butter and ½ cup powdered sugar in large bowl at medium speed of electric mixer until light and fluffy. Gradually add 1 cup flour, vanilla and salt. Beat at low speed until well blended. Stir in remaining 1 cup flour and ground nuts with spoon. Shape dough into ball; wrap in plastic wrap and refrigerate 1 hour or until firm.

3. Preheat oven to 350°F. Shape dough into 1-inch balls. Place 1 inch apart on ungreased cookie sheets.

4. Bake 12 to 15 minutes or until lightly browned. Let cookies stand on cookie sheets 2 minutes.

5. Meanwhile, place 1 cup powdered sugar in 13×9-inch glass dish. Transfer hot cookies to powdered sugar. Roll cookies in powdered sugar, coating well. Let cookies cool in sugar.

6. Sift remaining ½ cup powdered sugar over sugar-coated cookies before serving. Store tightly covered at room temperature or freeze up to 1 month.

MEXICAN WEDDING COOKIES

CHOCOLATE-RUM PARFAITS

Makes 4 servings

- 6 to 6½ ounces **Mexican chocolate, coarsely chopped***
- 1½ cups **whipping cream, divided**
- 3 tablespoons **golden rum (optional)**
- ¾ teaspoon **vanilla**
  - **Additional whipped cream, for garnish**
  - **Sliced almonds, for garnish**
  - **Cookies (optional)**

Or, substitute 6 ounces semisweet chocolate, coarsely chopped, 1 tablespoon ground cinnamon and ¼ teaspoon almond extract for Mexican chocolate.

1. Combine chocolate and 3 tablespoons cream in top of double boiler. Heat over simmering water until chocolate is melted and smooth, stirring occasionally. Gradually stir in rum, if desired; remove top pan from heat. Let stand at room temperature 15 minutes to cool slightly.

2. Combine remaining cream and vanilla in chilled deep bowl. Beat at low speed of electric mixer; gradually increase speed until stiff, but not dry, peaks form.

3. Gently fold whipped cream into cooled chocolate mixture until uniform in color. Spoon chocolate mixture into 4 individual dessert dishes. Refrigerate 2 to 3 hours until firm. Garnish with additional whipped cream and sliced almonds. Serve with cookies, if desired.

CHOCOLATE-RUM PARFAITS

NEW MEXICAN HOT CHOCOLATE

Makes 4 servings

- ¼ cup unsweetened cocoa powder
- ¼ cup sugar
- ½ teaspoon ground cinnamon
- ¼ teaspoon ground nutmeg
  Dash salt
- ⅔ cup water
- 3⅓ cups milk
- 1 teaspoon vanilla
- 4 cinnamon sticks or dash ground nutmeg

Combine cocoa, sugar, ground cinnamon, ¼ teaspoon nutmeg, salt and water in large saucepan. Cook, stirring occasionally, over medium heat until cocoa and sugar are dissolved. Add milk and vanilla. Heat to simmering. Whip mixture with electric mixer until frothy. Pour into four mugs. Place one cinnamon stick in each mug or sprinkle with nutmeg.

BISCOCHITOS

Makes 4 to 5 dozen cookies

- 3 cups all-purpose flour
- 2 teaspoons anise seeds
- 1½ teaspoons baking powder
- ½ teaspoon salt
- 1 cup (2 sticks) butter
- ¾ cup sugar, divided
- 1 egg
- ¼ cup orange juice
- 2 teaspoons ground cinnamon

1. Preheat oven to 350°F. Combine flour, anise seeds, baking powder and salt in medium bowl; set aside. Beat butter in large bowl at medium speed of electric mixer until creamy. Add ½ cup sugar; beat until fluffy. Blend in egg. Gradually add flour mixture alternately with orange juice, mixing well after each addition.

2. Divide dough in half. Roll out one portion at a time on lightly floured surface to ¼-inch thickness; cover remaining dough to prevent drying. Cut out cookies with cookie cutters 2- to 2½ inches in diameter, gather remaining scraps and reroll. If dough becomes too soft to handle, refrigerate briefly. Place cookies 1 inch apart on ungreased cookie sheets.

3. Combine remaining ¼ cup sugar and cinnamon; lightly sprinkle over cookies. Bake 8 to 10 minutes or until edges are lightly browned. Remove to wire racks; cool completely. Store in airtight containers.

Top to bottom: New Mexican Hot Chocolate and Biscochitos

MEXICAN SUGAR COOKIES (POLVORONES)

Makes about 2 dozen cookies

- **1 cup (2 sticks) butter, softened**
- **½ cup powdered sugar**
- **2 tablespoons milk**
- **1 teaspoon vanilla**
- **1 teaspoon ground cinnamon, divided**
- **1½ to 1¾ cups all-purpose flour**
- **1 teaspoon baking powder**
- **1 cup granulated sugar**
- **1 square (1 ounce) semisweet chocolate, finely grated**

1. Preheat oven to 325°F. Grease cookie sheets; set aside.

2. Beat butter, powdered sugar, milk, vanilla and ½ teaspoon cinnamon in large bowl at medium speed of electric mixer until light and fluffy, scraping down side of bowl once. Gradually add 1½ cups flour and baking powder. Beat at low speed until well blended, scraping down side of bowl once. Stir in additional flour with spoon if dough is too soft to shape.

3. Roll tablespoonfuls of dough into 1¼-inch balls. Place balls 3 inches apart on prepared cookie sheets. Flatten each ball into 2-inch round with bottom of glass dipped in granulated sugar.

4. Bake 20 to 25 minutes or until edges are golden brown. Let stand on cookie sheets 3 to 4 minutes.

5. Meanwhile, combine granulated sugar, grated chocolate and remaining ½ teaspoon cinnamon in small bowl. Transfer cookies, one at a time to sugar mixture; coat both sides. Remove to wire racks; cool completely.

6. Store tightly covered at room temperature or freeze up to 3 months.

MEXICAN SUGAR COOKIES (POLVORONES)

HONEY SOPAIPILLAS

Makes 16 sopaipillas

> ¼ **cup plus 2 teaspoons sugar, divided**
> ½ **teaspoon ground cinnamon**
> 2 **cups all-purpose flour**
> ½ **teaspoon salt**
> 2 **teaspoons baking powder**
> 2 **tablespoons shortening**
> ¾ **cup warm water**
> **Vegetable oil for deep-frying**
> **Honey**

1. Combine ¼ cup sugar and cinnamon in small bowl; set aside. Combine remaining 2 teaspoons sugar, flour, salt and baking powder in large bowl. Add shortening. With fingers, pastry blender or 2 knives, rub or cut in shortening until mixture resembles fine crumbs. Gradually add water; stir with fork until mixture forms dough. Turn out onto lightly floured board; knead 2 minutes or until smooth. Shape into a ball; cover with bowl and let rest 30 minutes.

2. Divide dough into 4 equal portions; shape each into a ball. Flatten each ball to form circle about 8 inches in diameter and ⅛ inch thick. Cut each round into 4 wedges.

3. Pour oil into electric skillet or deep heavy pan to depth of 1½ inches. Heat to 360°F. Cook dough, 2 pieces at a time, 2 minutes or until puffed and golden brown, turning once during cooking. Remove from oil with slotted spoon; drain on paper towels. Sprinkle with cinnamon-sugar mixture. Repeat with remaining sopaipillas. Serve hot with honey.

SANGRITA

Makes 6 (6-ounce) servings

> 3 **cups DEL MONTE® Tomato Juice**
> 1½ **cups orange juice**
> ½ **cup salsa**
> **Juice of 1 medium lime**

1. Mix all ingredients in large pitcher; chill.

2. Serve over ice with fruit garnishes, if desired.

Prep Time: 3 minutes

acknowledgments

The publisher would like to thank the companies and organizations listed below for the use of their recipes and photographs in this publication.

Campbell Soup Company

Del Monte Corporation

Grandma's® is a registered trademark of Mott's, Inc.

Guiltless Gourmet®

Heinz North America

The Kingsford Products Company

McIlhenny Company (TABASCO® brand Pepper Sauce)

National Chicken Council / US Poultry & Egg Association

National Pork Board

Ortega®

Reckitt Benckiser Inc.

index